Prayerful Pieces

Prayerful Pieces

Storied Moments of Tending the Heart

Hannah B. Johnson

Cover Art by Terrie Starkey

Charleston, SC
www.PalmettoPublishing.com

Prayerful Pieces

Copyright © 2021 by Hannah B. Johnson

All rights reserved.

No portion of this book may be reproduced, stored in a retrieval system, or transmitted in any form by any means–electronic, mechanical, photocopy, recording, or other–except for brief quotations in printed reviews, without prior permission of the author.

First Edition

Paperback ISBN: 978-1-63837-540-1

Table of Contents

Preface vii

    Moment 1 1
    Moment 2 6
    Moment 3 9
    Moment 4 12
    Moment 5 15
    Moment 6 18
    Moment 7 21
    Moment 8 24
    Moment 9 27
    Moment 10 30
    Moment 11 33
    Moment 12 36
    Moment 13 40
    Moment 14 44
    Moment 15 46
    Moment 16 49
    Moment 17 52
    Moment 18 54
    Moment 19 56
    Moment 20 60

Afterward 63

Discussion Guide 65

Acknowledgments 79

Preface

Why now?

I asked this with sincerity and from a place of utter exhaustion. How could I take on such a thoughtful task in a time where I rarely finished a thought?

Driving down the road, I cried out to the Lord to tell Him how busy I was, how worn I was, how unholy I was. I sought direction and permission to wait longer to fulfill this instruction laid firmly in my heart nearly three years before.

The day drove on and bedtime was turbulent. The echoes of crying children and requests for one last sip of water kept the silence I hungered for just out of my reach. I fell asleep heavy with hope of new mercy and the quiet of dawn ahead of me.

Lord, help me wake up and seek You.

The sun shone through the bedroom window and it was quiet. How long had it been since I had simply awoken without hearing my name?

It is a treasure to have a full home and life! It also comes at a cost: self. Even when I do my best at self-care and meet my needs, I still must sacrifice some of my wants to be the healthy, thoughtful mother and wife I aspire to be. I want to wake up in the quiet of morning to breathe before the busy day begins but, often, wet pajamas or hungry stomachs or excited giggles grace my bedside long before my alarm is set to awaken me.

On this quiet morning, I promptly arose from my bed. My bible and journal were already in their place on the side table. The room was tidy, thanks to a husband who knew it would matter. I sat down and asked the Lord again, *Why now?*

Pieces of Isaiah 40 repeated in my head. I opened the Word and read it again, finding fresh wind for my sails in each verse and pausing at the end.

> "He gives strength to the weary and increases the power of the weak. Even youths grow tired and weary, and young men stumble and fall; but those who hope in the Lord will renew their strength. They will soar on wings like eagles; they will run and not grow weary, they will walk and not be faint."
> Isaiah 40: 29-31

The image of Elijah, an old prophet who had just poured out his heart in grief and obedience to God, running ahead of a chariot for miles came to my mind.

> "The power of the Lord came on Elijah and, tucking his cloak into his belt, he ran ahead of Ahab all the way to Jezreel."
> 1 Kings 18:46

The Lord made it clear to me that now is His time so that I would always remember it was His power that brought forth this work. I'll tuck my proverbial cloak into my belt and start writing.

1

The cold clay mug fit snugly in her hand. She placed it back down on the wooden table amongst the colorful pottery for sale. The bustling market kept the warm day moving as people walked quickly from one market stall to the next.

She did her best to linger, to truly look for what she needed but also take notice of the hidden gems in this farmers' market. It was clean and well ordered. The vendors stood at the ready behind their stall tables. The produce was cool in the shade. Pottery and fragrant soaps often drew her gaze from her grocery list to the things she considered treasures.

Though this market had much to offer her, it was calm. The bustling about her, people moving from one space to the next, did not disturb the well-ordered layout of the market stalls or the gentleness of the vendors. Shoppers may have been in a rush but the market wasn't going anywhere on this warm, early morning.

What a contrast to the markets she had visited while on vacations or while on holidays in new places. Maybe it was the foreign nature of those markets that gave her a restlessness while shopping. Maybe it was the different market cultures—some vendors shouting after shoppers with prices to be won or bartered, while others sat indifferently reading newspapers.

Whatever the reason, she preferred her small town farmers' market. She walked back to her car with her canvas sack full and her heart at ease. The still-warm loaf of sourdough in her sack was ready to be sliced and covered with butter. She would see to that, shortly.

The toaster on the counter of her kitchen was her first stop at home. The television news was on in the background and her calm heart began to stir. She wanted to enjoy this morning, maybe spend some time in prayer and reading, but found the top stories that morning knocking around in her heart instead of informing her mind.

Lord, how can I stay informed but not become an unsettled mess? These stories break my heart and I believe they should! But why do they seem to steal my peace and disturb my spirit so much? I am taking action on what I can to serve You and the needs on that screen in my community. Praying is all I can do about the rest and You know I am doing that. I just can't take any more of these stations. Help me, Lord, to be informed but not disturbed.

The sourdough toast popped up and she reached for her butter knife. Her phone buzzed with a new message, someone needing something from her. She responded quickly on her way to her kitchen table. She just wanted to enjoy her toast in peace.

As she sat down, she considered her text response and realized it was not very gracious. There was no mercy in her words. Though she may have answered the question, she certainly didn't answer the person.

Lord, I can't believe that five minutes of news was all it took to undo my peace! It's been a long week but I thought this day was off to a great start. Father, forgive me and help me remain in your peace. Help me get to the root of my mess.

Almost instantly she placed her toast down and a scripture came to mind:

> "A good man brings good things out of the good stored up in his heart, and an evil man brings evil things out of the evil stored up in his heart. For the mouth speaks what the heart is full of."
> Luke 6:45

If my heart is a restless market, so will my words be. Lord, calm the market of my heart.

She pictured her heart: a temple of God surrounded by the warm, bustling market she had visited that morning in the bordering streets. The stalls were not vending soaps and sourdough, but freely tendering scripture and stories. She imagined that the people and circumstances she would encounter in her days would bustle through these outer courts of her heart. Her thoughtful words would come from different stalls.

It would take work in her heart to keep the stalls clean and ready. Even if no other person walked through her market, she would need this well ordered market to speak truth to herself.

What did her heart look like in that moment? Was it so misaligned with the purposes and truth of God that she should ask Jesus to come in flipping tables? Or was she needing careful handiwork to enter each stall with grace to set things right?

She imagined the stalls and began to write in her leather-bound notebook.

Here they are, Lord. The stalls of my heart (at least the ones I can understand now): Identity, Purpose, Love, Relationships, Marriage, Boundaries, Motherhood...

Her list continued in prayer and she found each stall would need routine care from the Lord who made them. She had learned about guarding her heart and that was essential to her!

> "Above all else, guard your heart, for everything you do flows from it."
> Proverbs 4:23

One must do that. But one must also care for what is in the heart. She was guarding her heart the best she could, but she knew she was not doing it perfectly. She must purify her heart from when the guarding slipped. She could not do that without the Lord. She had been in a wonderful community of godly women, but she needed alone time with God to do this heart tending, as well. She remembered an early lesson in faith—drawing near to God with the command to purify her heart:

> "Come near to God and he will come near to you. Wash your hands, you sinners, and purify your hearts, you double-minded."
> James 4:8

Lord, I am the last person that I need to be alone with. I speak lies to myself and often hurt myself more than anyone else could. I need more time alone with You. I do not need more time alone with my phone or the news or myself. I need You. This heart care can't happen without you. I'm ready, in Jesus' Name.

2

She thought he looked familiar. They looked at one another a few times before this boy across the aisle decidedly asked her name.

Moments later, they were whispering questions back and forth. The last time they sat side by side was at small elementary school desks, pouring glue onto their palms then watching it dry. Childhood classmates now reunited at a collective choral gathering of students from the mid-state region.

They were no longer gangly ten-year-olds, but seniors in high school. They both had determined their direction and were only eight months shy of stepping into, what they would call, adulthood.

Around the lunch table, their surface-level re-acquaintance took a sharp dive. He threw around the name "Jesus" with a boldness that unsettled but also engaged her. She watched her peers shudder and cringe at this new boy with a bold, unabashed faith.

They returned to their choral arrangements for three more hours of rehearsal. They had been singing these songs individually for months in preparation for this gathering but the words in the songs seemed to strike her differently that afternoon.

They sang, "Nicodemus was a man who desired to know how a man can be born when he's old. Christ told Nicodemus as a friend, 'Man, you must be born again' Said, 'Marvel not, man, if you wanna be wise, Repent, believe and be baptized'.... You'll be a witness for my Lord!" [1]

The score of the song struck uncomfortable notes in her heart. She had been praying to be closer to God the past few months but didn't know how. She cut her eyes over to the boy.

That's what a witness is. That's what this song is about. I believe. I am saved. But, he is a witness.

Their conversations continued in the rafters as they waited for their turn to perform that evening. She had nearly forgotten she was there with her peers from school. There was something striking that kept her leaning his direction to hear more.

"So, do you believe in Jesus?" he asked with that same, fervent boldness.

She firmly replied, "Yes, I do. I am saved. I believe."

He grinned and leaned back in the rafter pew. "Wow, I couldn't tell."

As much as she wanted to be angry and come up with some quip to put him in his place, she had nothing but appreciation for him in her heart.

---

1 Halloran, Jack. "Witness." *Traditional Spiritual.* Gentry Publications, 1986.

Someone had seen through her. She would later know that this boy was just following the moment-by-moment prompts of the Holy Spirit to answer a prayer in her heart to be nearer to God.

"Why not?" she asked, with honest searching in her eyes.

They took the few moments they had left together to discuss what behaviors and symptoms of salvation were missing from her life. He softened his voice and gently rebuked her for her foul language and rude jokes. He even guessed at a few deeper sins she thought were well hidden. He showed her that sin did not define her. She was quiet.

Moments later, they were standing back on the stage singing the last notes in a chorus of hundreds of other students.

"My soul is a witness for my Lord!" rang out from her mouth and, for the first time that day, from her heart.

Something had changed.

> "But as for me, it is good to be near God. I have made the Sovereign LORD my refuge; I will tell of all your deeds."
>
> Psalm 73:28

3

In spite of myself, Lord, please use me for your kingdom moment by moment.

She had poured out her heart to her dear friend. This was a safe place to confess her sins and trust that she would not be hushed back into the excuses that would fuel her poor choices. This was the kind of friendship that heard the sin, encouraged repentance, and spurred her on in the right direction.

This was also a gracious friend. She was swiftly reminded that trying to please the Father is way easier than trying to please man. The Father is gracious and merciful while holy and just. He is miraculously all of Himself all at once.

Her friend spoke into the phone with such gravity, crossing the hundreds of miles between them, "We grieve over our sin and repent of our fleshly desires but we *walk* powerfully in the Spirit as God has called us to walk."

She knew this was true. Though feeling a mess of fatigue and life's demands, she knew God was at work in her life. The encouragements of others confounded her as she often found herself inwardly focused on her own flaws.

Oh Lord God, help me to see what You see in me? Help me to understand what you are doing in and through me?

A new view of herself took shape as she prayerfully inventoried her life. She spoke words outwardly with a strength that she didn't recognize as she looked within. She walked with a boldness that must have come from the Lord directly.

Christ was at work in and through her. It felt almost as if He was taking her hand and leading her, just steps ahead of her. Those around her saw her face and heard her words only in the warmth of His light, the reflection of His glory strong in her countenance and speech.

The words of the apostle Paul now rang in her ears:

> "But he said to me, 'My grace is sufficient for you, for my power is made perfect in weakness.' Therefore I will boast all the more gladly about my weaknesses, so that Christ's power may rest on me."
> 2 Corinthians 12:9

She shared this scripture with her friend and they encouraged one another. They shared their joys and their trials, vowing to pray for one another. They boasted in their weaknesses with an expectation of God to transform and empower them. She went to her knees in prayer.

I am not what people need, Lord God. May Christ increase in me as I decrease? May He be the peace that leads me and the power that sustains me? In Jesus' Name, Amen.

4

Taking advantage of the moment, she reached for the phone to make the only important call on her to-do list that day. These windows of quiet were few and far between. She acted quickly.

"Thank you for calling. How may I assist you today?" chimed the helpful attendant on the other end of the line.

She went on with her purpose for calling, explaining what she needed. She enjoyed the kindness of the woman attending her needs. It was only a minute into the call that a very upset child rounded the corner.

Pulling at her clothes and crying in frustration, the child detailed the offenses of her sibling. The kind attendant on the line asked for a moment to work on her task. She now had a momentary window to look her child in the eyes.

She listened as the child presented the case against her sibling, with self defense found mingled in for good measure.

"Okay, I do understand. She hurt you and you reacted but you don't get to hurt someone else just because you are hurt. In your anger, do not sin. Being angry is not a sin but the things you did because you were angry are. Please have a seat and I can help you in just a moment."

She watched her child walk to the bench beside her and take a seat, frustrated but not surprised at her mother's reaction. She suddenly realized she was still on the phone.

"I'm sorry. I'm back now, if you are ready to keep going."

The attendant was quick and clearly had been listening in, "Say that again! Really, tell me what you told her! I need to hear it."

She repeated her admonishment just as she had said it to her child then added, "The Bible says in Ephesians 4:26, '"In your anger do not sin": Do not let the sun go down while you are still angry,' and I remind my kiddos that it is okay to be angered but not to let that lead to sin. Sin would be feeling or acting in a way that goes against God, His character, or His law."

"Whew, I needed that. That is good! Like, I needed to go to church and you took me there!" the attendant exclaimed with a true appreciation.

In all honesty, she had at first been frustrated that her call was interrupted and even more so embarrassed that she had to discipline her child in the midst of this task. The smile crossing her face now reminded her of further truth from her Savior.

"And we know that in all things God works for the good of those who love him, who have been called according to his purpose."
Romans 8:38

Thank you, Lord, that nothing is wasted in your economy. You are steady and resourceful - truly full of every resource and effortlessly able to assign it to where it is needed. Thank you for reminding me to be faithful in every moment with both the tasks I expect and the unexpected. I just love you, Lord.

5

"May I hang this poster here for our church play?"

She had just entered the small donut shop. It was one of her many stops as she canvassed the neighborhood with the church advertisement. She was hoping and praying that many would come and be moved by the message in this play.

The young girl, not more than 17 years old, looked up at her and said, "Sure! Hang it over there above the garbage can and napkins. Nobody will miss it!"

"Well thank you," she said. "What do I owe you for hanging the sign?"

The girl at the counter shook her head and said, "Oh nothing! In fact, would you like to take a couple of dozen glazed donuts with you? I'm about to close up for the night and there are no charities picking up our leftovers this weekend."

The last thing she needed was two dozen donuts but she hesitantly said yes, knowing her children would love them. She asked, "Are you sure? Is there anything I can do for you in return?"

"No, seriously I'm about to throw them all into the garbage. Just take them!" the young girl responded.

She found it hard to believe that that many donuts would be going straight into the trash but knew that day-old donuts are not that good so she made a mental note to make sure her family knew about the treats she would leave on the kitchen counter for the morning.

Looking back up to the young girl across the extended boxes, she said matter-of-factly, "Well then, I will just pray for you instead."

The girl drew back her own hands and placed them at her side mumbling thank you and looking visibly awkward about her offer. She turned to leave the shop and made a mental note to pray for this young girl working the late shift at a donut shop. When she got to her van she placed her donuts inside and turned back around to look at the girl now sweeping the floor behind the donut counter. Why wait to pray?

Father God, thank You for letting me meet this young girl tonight. Thank you for her kindness and generosity. I pray that she would know You. I pray that she would love and follow after Jesus. Father, draw her near to You and rid her of all that keeps her from walking with You. Bless her with joy and boldness, with peace and strength. In the name of Jesus I pray, Amen.

By the end of her prayer, the young girl had looked up and noticed her standing at the van. The girl did not look away, but watched as she finished her silent prayer, got back into the van, and drove off. She wouldn't know on this side of heaven the results of her prayer that night but she believed it would be fruitful. And it was.

> "Therefore confess your sins to each other and pray for each other so that you may be healed. The prayer of a righteous person is powerful and effective."
> James 5:16

6

"It would be better to be homeless and know Jesus than to have a safe home and be apart from him," explained the speaker. [2]

This was the loudest part of the message ringing in her mind after the speaker shared a powerful testimony of deliverance from human trafficking and abuse. During a prayer event simulcast to women all over the world, the speaker shared about the moment Jesus met her in a prison cell.

How many people do I know that would rather know You and be homeless than to have a home apart from You?

The excitement and passion that so many Christians display when they first know Christ—that urgency to tell everyone and make clear His importance in their lives—still poured out of the speaker years after her conversion. It was a challenge to the "settled" in their faith who slowly lose that passion or become burdened over time by all of the extra baggage we pick up along the way.

---

2 Christa Lynn, She Loves Out Loud, 15 February 2020, USA. Simulcast Conference.

She found herself crying in the wooden church pew because she was not sure how many people she knew that felt the way the speaker described.

Has Jesus become, in my life, less essential or less desirable than the comforts of a safe home, steady job, or consistent schedule? What about the lives of my friends? My family? My church?

The warning came in loud and clear to her soul—her Joy was in Jesus Christ, but, if she let her gaze slip from His face, then she would find herself prizing other things above Him. She could end up, not only less passionate about telling others about Him, but also believing things about Jesus that were not true of Him.

> "I, even I, am the Lord,
>   and apart from me there is no savior.
> I have revealed and saved and proclaimed—
>   I, and not some foreign god among you.
> You are my witnesses," declares the Lord, "that I am God.
>   Yes, and from ancient days I am he.
> No one can deliver out of my hand.
>   When I act, who can reverse it?"
>   Isaiah 43:11-13

She turned to the Word and found God, unchanging and alive, was who He said He was. He always had been and always would be Himself.

Lord, thank you for renewing my passion for salvation! Thank you for saving me, in spite of myself. You love me and I love you. I am devoted to You. Help me know You for Who You are and not who I want You to be. When I hear someone speak of You, make it clear to me if it is really You they know and speak of. Help me test and discern every spirit I meet.

"Dear friends, do not believe every spirit, but test the spirits to see whether they are from God, because many false prophets have gone out into the world. This is how you can recognize the Spirit of God: Every spirit that acknowledges that Jesus Christ has come in the flesh is from God, but every spirit that does not acknowledge Jesus is not from God. This is the spirit of the antichrist, which you have heard is coming and even now is already in the world.

You, dear children, are from God and have overcome them, because the one who is in you is greater than the one who is in the world. They are from the world and therefore speak from the viewpoint of the world, and the world listens to them. We are from God, and whoever knows God listens to us; but whoever is not from God does not listen to us. This is how we recognize the Spirit of truth and the spirit of falsehood."
1 John 4:1-6

7

They walked through the doors together and paused. She looked over her right shoulder. *Just look my way once*, her heart pleaded through her tearless glance.

Fighting for something that seemed nonexistent had left her with a hole in her chest she could almost feel with her hands. She felt as though she could fold into this crater and disappear completely as she waited one moment more for a response from him.

Nothing. No shrug of indifference. No steely glare back in her direction. Did he know her eyes were searching his face for a glimmer of hope?

If he did, maybe it was defiance that kept his gaze fixed forward. Her mind began to race with thoughts she imagined in his head. *He must hate me. He must think I am as unlovable as I feel. He must....*

She found herself minutes into this spiral of wandering thoughts. They did not talk anymore. The lack of communication left her filling in the gaps just like this. To her mind, he had become a person of her own creation.

Where do I go from here, Lord? This isn't some stranger on the street. This is my person. I don't want to walk away but I can't live like this anymore.

"Above all, love each other deeply, because love covers over a multitude of sins." 1 Peter 4:8

She balked in prayer, *How? It isn't that simple, Father. What does it even mean to love in this moment?*

> "Love is patient, love is kind. It does not envy, it does not boast, it is not proud. It does not dishonor others, it is not self-seeking, it is not easily angered, it keeps no record of wrongs. Love does not delight in evil but rejoices with the truth. It always protects, always trusts, always hopes, always perseveres."
> 1 Corinthians 13:4-7

In this new light, their wedding played in her mind. The pastor read these passages, telling them that this love was for all believers toward one another. This love is what tells the world that followers of Jesus are different; that despite their differences and grievances, unity was still possible. This love, especially within a marriage, should nourish and sustain a union far beyond what mere men could try to keep together.

> "Love never fails. But where there are prophecies, they will cease; where there are tongues, they will be stilled; where there is knowledge, it will pass away. For we know in part and we prophesy in part, but when completeness comes, what is in part disappears.

When I was a child, I talked like a child, I thought like a child, I reasoned like a child. When I became a man, I put the ways of childhood behind me. For now we see only a reflection as in a mirror; then we shall see face to face. Now I know in part; then I shall know fully, even as I am fully known. And now these three remain: faith, hope and love. But the greatest of these is love."
1 Corinthians 13:8-13

Though you know me completely, Lord God, I only know You in part for now. Help me know You more. Make me like You, Lord. I only know him in part but You, God, know him completely. Make a way for us to know one another again.

For the first time in weeks, she breathed in hope. It wasn't much hope, but it was just enough.

8

The headlights coming towards her in her own lane quickly awakened her muscles to act. Muscle memory sneaks in at the best and worst of times. The drizzling rain and cold wind had fooled her eyes in the dark of evening.

That's the wrong side of the road, girl!, she said to herself.

As her car quickly entered the right side of the road, she felt the tears welling up in her eyes. This reminded her that she had a home, once, far away. She'd not just been a visitor but a resident. She had owned a car and bought her groceries, folded laundry and tended to children's needs in a country far away from the one in which she now resided.

She found herself setting up life in a new town. Was it time to buy all she needed in bulk instead of the small or travel size options? Would she be here long enough for her muscles to remember the roads?

She did hope so. She was happy with hope while still hurting with yearning for a different kind of music and a different shade of greenery.

A scripture crossed her mind as she pondered how she was meant to live amidst a world that seemed satisfied apart from God –

> "Dear friends, I urge you, as foreigners and exiles, to abstain from sinful desires, which wage war against your soul."
> 1 Peter 2:11

Oh, Lord, this world is not my home. Help me to live as a foreigner and quit searching for an eternal home amongst these temporary places. Keep my grasp on my earthly belongings and treasures loose and liberated.

It seemed that so many people she loved and knew were living within miles of their homeplace—another generation of generations in the same place. That wasn't her life. That wasn't her story. She found herself far from the place she was raised and embracing a culture different from her own.

What a mystery that some would be called to stay and others to leave. She had to embrace the reality that those staying on their native soil were called to do so in the same way she was called to be elsewhere. The temptation was often to look on at the person who seems to be sacrificing so much stability to go wherever the Lord called them with more respect or admiration in this Kingdom of God.

Maybe she did feel that way once. Having lived this out, she found it no more pious to roam the earth obediently than to tend an established garden at home obediently. Often the ends of the earth are street corners at home.

> "So Christ himself gave the apostles, the prophets, the evangelists, the pastors and teachers, to equip his people for works of service, so that the body of Christ may be built up until we all reach unity in the faith and in the knowledge of the Son of God and become mature, attaining to the whole measure of the fullness of Christ."
> Ephesians 4:11-13

She fixed her hands on the steering wheel once more and thought, *Faithful obedience to God is everyone's calling. Everyone has his or her own part to play in this Kingdom. Lord, continue to show me what that looks like in my life.*

9

The kitchen window glistened with dewy drops focusing the morning light. Her exhaustion was felt from her head to her toes, cheeks tingling and shoulders aching as she filled the coffee pot. She thought, *I am not enough.*

No matter how many quotes or blogs seemed to say that she was, she felt utterly and completely insufficient for the many tasks that would land in her hands that day. She strived to fulfill her duties day in and day out but still fell asleep acutely aware of each moment in which she had not met the mark. Not one of her offerings seemed to fulfill their purpose.

Water dripped down the side of the coffee pot as she poured the water into the reservoir. Another day was starting with its first mess to clean as the water pooled on the counter. She swiped the hand towel over the pool and pressed start on the coffee maker. The promise of coffee offered a momentary relief.

I am not enough, Lord.

One sentence of prayer and she was washed over with a warm wave of spiritual relief: She did not have to be enough. She never had to be enough. She found no place in the Word that asked her to be enough for anything or anyone. God was not asking her to be enough. She found that He was simply asking her to be willing.

Willing to what, Lord?

She remembered Abraham on his way to do what seemed the hardest thing he would ever do: sacrifice his own son, Isaac. She envisioned this moment as the father leads his son up a mountain with all the supplies for a sacrifice but no animal in sight. At the moment of sacrifice, the angel of the Lord God calls out to rescue Isaac. She believed that Abraham was willing to come to that moment because he *knew* the God asking this task of him.

> "Abraham looked up and there in a thicket he saw a ram caught by its horns. He went over and took the ram and sacrificed it as a burnt offering instead of his son. So Abraham called that place The Lord Will Provide. And to this day it is said, "On the mountain of the Lord it will be provided.""
> Genesis 22:13-14

Oh, what a willingness to trust God with each next step! What a treasure to know He would show up in her time of need because He placed her right there! Could she be willing to press on in pursuit of God's call on her life? To live her life for His glory, and not her own?

You are Yahweh Jireh, the Lord will see and see to it. You are the Lord who provides. I don't have to be enough because You are and know all I need.

"And whatever you do, whether in word or deed, do it all in the name of the Lord Jesus, giving thanks to God the Father through him."
                              Colossians 3:17

10

Her child moaned loudly and yelled, "Next things are hard!"

The progression from doing well-known tasks to learning a new level of skills was more than the child could take at that moment. She got down on the ground beside the child, sprawled out of control.

She took her child's face in her hands and gently said, "Next things are hard but you are not doing them alone."

The child crumbled into her arms with relief and more tears flowed. In her mother's lap, the child wept and detailed all that was bottled up behind the facade of hatred for arithmetic. There was so much more concerning her child's heart than she had expected to learn. The next things were not just fractions but so much deeper.

Lord, I'm not sure I'm ready for the next things. I don't have the words to process these feelings for myself, let alone walk her through them.

Her own admonishments to her child seemed whispered back in her own ear, "Next things are hard but you are not doing them alone."

She spoke into her child's ear, "You don't have to figure these feelings out alone. I am here and, more importantly, God is with us both. Let's pray for help and maybe things will make more sense."

This was not the first time a child of God would balk incredulously at the thought of doing what God had given them to do. Finding the words for a child's aching heart seemed especially hard when she hadn't quite figured out how to speak the truth she needed to her own heart yet.

She thought of Moses. God chose to appear to him in such an unbelievable way and with a command that would confront turmoil within him that he was avoiding at great lengths. Tending to sheep far from his home in Egypt, God finds him to show him he is not alone. The Lord answered each question Moses presented and, in doing so, provided the counsel Moses needed to heal his wounds.

Moses's penultimate request to be excused from the duties God had given him was held on his inability to speak. God provided an answer but not about Moses himself. The answer to Moses's inability to speak depended not on Moses but on the God that was calling him.

> "The Lord said to him, 'Who gave human beings their mouths? Who makes them deaf or mute? Who gives them sight or makes them blind? Is it not I, the Lord? Now go; I will help you speak and will teach you what to say.'"
>
> Exodus 4:11-12

Jesus spoke similarly to his disciples as they prepared to face persecution (Mark 13:11). Again, Christ assured them of His presence, knowing they would go to tell the world about Him (Matthew 28). She spoke the same to her hurting child in an equally daunting task: speaking truth to herself.

> "...And surely I am with you always, to the very end of the age."
> Matthew 28:20b

11

Still moist from the morning dew, the grass soaked her shirt and the bottoms of her feet as she lay under the poplar tree. Big strong branches reached out wider than the shade the tree was providing.

To her side was a friend who laughed and giggled with her as they talked about what it would be like to be women one day. They imagined long dresses with shoes that would make them inches taller than their mothers. They talked about husbands and babies. They wondered what work would occupy their time. They tried not to wonder if they would still be the best of friends.

How far away those days were! It seemed it would take them 100 years to bridge the gap from 12 to 20 years old.

They didn't know how swiftly the years would go or how this treasured childhood friendship would help establish their goals for sisterhood in the future. Years later, she would think of this friend when reading the Bible's verses on faithfulness, love, and honor.

The beauty of this childhood friendship, held together with a child-like faith under a poplar tree, would help her be the friend others would need. It would help her stand up for the bullied girl in university. It would remind her she was valued when a woman dismissed her in the church lobby. It would warm her face with a smile as she looked on at her newborn daughter.

Play yard daydreams would be realized and, though this particular friendship was more of a memory, those two girls under the poplar tree would each save a fond place for the years behind them in their hearts. What an impact a friend can make.

She sat watching her daughter play with a new friend. Now, as a grown woman, she thought of how much etiquette and thoughtfulness is developed in the playtime of children. Her daughter's nervousness was clear as the girl shared a story with her new friend.

She did not know what was being said, but saw the searching look for approval on her daughter's face. The new friend smiled and received the whispered words with acceptance, while relief washed over her daughter. A high five sealed the moment and the two children were off to their next task of play.

Lord, give them grace and love for one another. May they confide in one another and spur one another on toward goodness and grace. Give them deep, true friendship.

Though this was a prayer for her daughter's new friendship, she had often prayed the same over her own. There was just no place for anything less than true friendship in the busy days of life.

Behold, how good and pleasant it is
when brothers dwell in unity!
It is like the precious oil on the head,
running down on the beard,
on the beard of Aaron,
running down on the collar of his robes!
It is like the dew of Hermon,
which falls on the mountains of Zion!
For there the Lord has commanded the blessing,
life forevermore.
Psalm 133: 1-3

12

It was the greatest compromise of her young life. Where would she go from here?

She thought back to that moment she first believed in the Lord. Having known or sensed God was real from her early memories as a child, she sat on the shaky wooden bench at Bible camp with much knowledge in her head but little in her heart.

She tried her best to sing along to songs everyone there knew so well. Her family hadn't been regularly in church for years. These were not songs she would have known from any church she attended. By the end of the week, she had learned one very well. When it came time for it, she sat a little taller and readied herself to sing.

"You are Holy. You are mighty. You are worthy, worthy of praise. I will follow. I will listen. I will love you all of my days."[3]

---

3 Michael W. Smith. Lyrics to "You Are Holy (Prince of Peace)." *Genius*, 2021, https://genius.com/Michaelw-smith-you-are-holyprince-of-peace-lyrics.

A warm breeze lifted the thick curly hair from her neck. She looked up into the oak tree above her and knew: He is who He says He is, this Jesus.

God, I don't know if I believe everything these people here are saying, but I believe in You. I believe in Jesus, and I know I need Him. Forgive me and make me new.

Fresh wind and breath graced her and she knew she was saved.

It only made sense that, in the shadow of her greatest compromise of character and morals, she would consider that moment. She quickly dialed her closest friend and hoped for an answer on the first ring.

"Hey, girl. What's up?"

She spilled every detail and burden on her heart into the eager ear of her friend. She knew this friend did not follow Jesus, but, quite frankly, she knew few other believers. She was at a loss for how to repent and was too ashamed to talk with family.

"Well, you didn't get struck by lightning, so God must be alright with you! Give yourself a break. This is not that bad. Life happens. Let's go get…" her friend continued.

The plans trailed on and she felt a brief relief, but, as she lay in bed that night, she knew this was what sin felt like. A conviction she could not explain gripped her gut. She would ignore it for months… then years.

It was hard to admit her actions went against the God who made and saved her. It was even harder when the people around her saw her actions as permissible or good for her self-esteem. The conviction she wanted to hide was quickly covered by the praises of an unbelieving crowd.

One day, years later, she read the words of a Puritan and understood them to her very core.

> ...take heed thou speakest not peace to thyself before God speaks it; but hearken what he says to thy soul. ...It is a sad thing for a man to deceive his own soul herein. All the warnings God gives us, in tenderness to our souls, to try and examine ourselves, do tend to the preventing of this great evil of speaking peace groundlessly to ourselves; which is upon the issue to bless ourselves, in opposition to God.
> John Owen, The Mortification of Sin[4]

Though language had changed between the 1650s and the early 2000s, the soul's tendency to work it's way out of the holy convictions of God had not. Quieting conviction—speaking peace to our souls when we actually need repentance—appeared even easier to her as the world around her affirmed all she felt convicted to cast off.

Be it an unbelieving friend or a gracious sister in Christ, peace had been spoken to her sinfulness more times than she could remember. That great, wounding compromise in her adolescence no more warranted inappropriate peace to assuage it than the small, daily compromises in her adult years.

No sin, no matter its size or quality, should be permitted, but instead should lead to repentance—admitting the sin and turning

---

[4] Owen, John. *The Mortification of Sin*. Presbyterian Board of Publication, 1880.

away from it completely to walk in the way of Christ. Grace abounds for such moments, and she vowed never to forget it.

> Do not offer any part of yourself to sin as an instrument of wickedness, but rather offer yourselves to God as those who have been brought from death to life; and offer every part of yourself to him as an instrument of righteousness. For sin shall no longer be your master, because you are not under the law, but under grace.
> Romans 6:13-14

> As obedient children, do not conform to the evil desires you had when you lived in ignorance. But just as he who called you is holy, so be holy in all you do; for it is written: 'Be holy, because I am holy.'
> 1 Peter 1:14-16

13

She turned the phone over, unable to look at the words on its screen.

Tears rolled down her cheeks. Severing ties with someone she loved seemed like the only next step. Chance after chance had been offered to this person who continually wounded her.

The phone buzzed again on the desk below. How can the words that give life be used to defend or inflict injury after injury?

She hesitated to pick it up, so many tasks being laid aside so that she could truly read the messages flying in from the fingertips of a loved one.

Accusations pierced her heart, one letter at a time, with their half-truths and calls to repentance. Each sentence seemed more intense and damning while the Word she loved was used to shame and accuse her.

She had never thought of herself in these terms—the words glaring off her screen. She wondered if maybe this loved one was right. Was she the person described in each message? Where was the truth in any of this?

She started to reply. Her words now failed her. There was no way to win. Keeping it simple, she tried to end the barrage with a clear-cut goodbye. There was work to do and people to care for, leaving no time for tearful texting today.

A wise man later told her that it's a lot easier to talk to someone when you decide you don't have to be right. It was a sentiment that brought her back to this conversation. She didn't feel the need to be right—what a relief! She did feel a burden to stand up for truth. But, how could she?

A few deep breaths and tissues later, she went to people she trusted. She took the words on her phone and the words still bound in her heart to people who knew her, and a few who didn't. Each counselor helped her see the truth through the texts, cleaning the wounds those words had inflicted and offering a salve to help heal what now needed bandaging. She prayed and asked God for clarity.

She went to the Word in prayer. *Father, please help me. You know me. Nobody knows me like You do. Who am I? Help me repent and help me forgive.*

> Finally, be strong in the Lord and in his mighty power. Put on the full armor of God, so that you can take your stand against the devil's schemes. For our struggle is not against flesh and blood, but against the rulers, against the authorities, against the powers of this dark world and against the spiritual forces of evil in the heavenly realms. Therefore put on the full armor

of God, so that when the day of evil comes, you may be able to stand your ground, and after you have done everything, to stand. Stand firm then, with the belt of truth buckled around your waist, with the breastplate of righteousness in place, and with your feet fitted with the readiness that comes from the gospel of peace. In addition to all this, take up the shield of faith, with which you can extinguish all the flaming arrows of the evil one. Take the helmet of salvation and the sword of the Spirit, which is the word of God. And pray in the Spirit on all occasions with all kinds of prayers and requests. With this in mind, be alert and always keep on praying for all the Lord's people.
Ephesians 6:10-18

Oh, how she needed this Word. The Word of God—the Bible, the Son in script—that is the sword of the Spirit of God. She grasped the Word in her hands and her heart. She saw that a sword, while powerfully effective in the hands of a trained warrior, can do damage when taken up incorrectly.

Whether hands are unfit for this sword for lack of practice or strength, it is certain that a poorly wielded sword may wound but not achieve its true purpose. "For our struggle is not against flesh and blood..." rang in the halls of her mind as she saw the Word afresh.

The Word of God seemed purposed as a warrior's weapon against the spiritual enemies of God while also a surgeon's scalpel toward the flesh of His children.

> For the word of God is alive and active. Sharper than any double-edged sword, it penetrates even to dividing soul and spirit, joints and marrow; it judges the thoughts and attitudes of the heart.
> Hebrews 4:12

How many times had she seen men take up the sword of the Spirit to stab a son in the back or cut down a daughter doing her best to stand firm?

She turned back to the Lord in prayer, *May Your Word do its task in me, and may my hands be able to wield this sword only as You direct me.*

14

It didn't matter that the room was dimly lit or that the heat was out. Her cold fingers worked hard to form each chord on her worn guitar neck. The few people gathered there sang with the fullness of joy she had not seen in a stadium full of believers.

The ease of their prayers and praise was magnified by the shared sense of God's presence with them. The Lord inhabited their praise. He was the melody to which they all sang.

Not only did their song rise together in unity, but their closeness spiritually felt otherworldly. She had only known them for such a short time but found herself perceiving the needs of those around her in a way nearly beyond her familial connections. This was reciprocated as near strangers prayed for her.

How do they know this about me, Lord? How can we, newly in this community, already be at such a depth of relationship?

She found her answer in the One who knew her: the Lord God. The God who knew her lived in those around her, as well. The very

Spirit of God was uniquely present in each of them individually and yet also in their midst simultaneously.

She nearly laughed out loud as she considered this. As she thought of how great God was, her joy bubbled over and she was warm hearted with delight. The chords of the song she played seemed an afterthought as she sat in that joy.

She lifted her eyes to the handful of people around her and knew they felt the same. The Lord was near! It was clear on the faces of all in the room. A simple meeting of prayer and praise turned into a holy moment, one she would reflect on often.

Lord, help me treasure You as my delight and my joy at all times. Place me in rooms like this, knowing and believing You with others who want the same.

> Be very careful, then, how you live—not as unwise but as wise, making the most of every opportunity, because the days are evil. Therefore do not be foolish, but understand what the Lord's will is. Do not get drunk on wine, which leads to debauchery. Instead, be filled with the Spirit, speaking to one another with psalms, hymns, and songs from the Spirit. Sing and make music from your heart to the Lord, always giving thanks to God the Father for everything, in the name of our Lord Jesus Christ.
> Ephesians 5:15-20

15

The mess of this fumbled work was everywhere. It wasn't just the stacks of papers and unsuccessful emails that were messy before her. The words already spoken and the feelings of the ones around her were a mess she felt ill equipped to clean up.

How did I do this, again? I try over and over to stay out of this situation, Lord. Somehow, I end up here again. Help me, Lord. How did I get here?

> "I am the vine; you are the branches. If you remain in me and I in you, you will bear much fruit; apart from me you can do nothing."
> John 15:5

The scripture echoed over the table covered in papers. Her good intentions and honest attempts to serve God lay there beneath a Truth unseen but surely felt.

You are right, Father. Show me where I have stepped out of Your desires for me. Help me tend to whatever is keeping me from abiding in You. Teach me to remain. In Jesus's Name, Amen.

She took a deep breath and started to file away the papers. She knew she would accomplish the most when she tended to the needs and contents of her heart in prayer, study, and time alone with God.

She had been doing this for years. She wondered when she would get it right instead of fumbling such important tasks. The chime of her phone brought her hands to a pause as she glanced at the words on its screen.

"Hey, it's a wild season but remember that you have more strengths than weaknesses! We all slip up and the Lord keeps us humble, friend. Take a break to rest in the Lord, today, and then keep walking in His strength and power. His grace covers you!"

This was the end of a long morning of messaging back and forth. She read the words and wanted to believe them. She did need a break.

I do need a break. Help me rest in you, today. Help me clear out this mess to make room for the Master—You, Lord Jesus.

With her papers filed and her computer set aside, she sat down on the couch to open the Word of God. She lifted the satin ribbon to the last scriptures she had been reading.

> Therefore, since we have been justified through faith, we have peace with God through our Lord Jesus Christ, through whom we have gained access by faith into this grace in which we now stand. And we boast in the hope of the glory of God. Not only so, but we also glory in our sufferings, because we know that suffering produces perseverance; perseverance, character; and character, hope. And hope does not put us to shame, because God's love has

been poured out into our hearts through the Holy Spirit, who has been given to us.

You see, at just the right time, when we were still powerless, Christ died for the ungodly. Very rarely will anyone die for a righteous person, though for a good person someone might possibly dare to die. But God demonstrates his own love for us in this: While we were still sinners, Christ died for us.

Since we have now been justified by his blood, how much more shall we be saved from God's wrath through him! For if, while we were God's enemies, we were reconciled to him through the death of his Son, how much more, having been reconciled, shall we be saved through his life! Not only is this so, but we also boast in God through our Lord Jesus Christ, through whom we have now received reconciliation.
Romans 5:1-11

The core of her faith lay written before her in her Bible. The tears poured from her eyes onto the pages. She was no longer sad or burdened but renewed and comforted! What a treasure to be loved by God! This would never be elementary for her; no matter how many years she had been working this faith out in action.

Centered and hopeful, she laid her open bible down before her. Prayers too deep for words poured from her spirit to her Father in heaven. This was good.

16

Will he love me, Lord? Will he love me and cherish me and make me feel this special forever?

The sting of past love and loss were still somewhat fresh. Some days they seemed to have faded completely and others it would hit her like a ton of bricks. Remembering those fears of never living up to what was expected of her, how she would look or behave, made her cautious to fall in love again.

She had only been walking with Jesus for a few months. She loved how secure she felt in Him and her identity as His beloved! To seek some kind of love or affection from a man now seemed a larger hurdle then she had anticipated.

He looked across the table at her with an innocent grin. He was funny. He made her laugh and that was a completely new feeling in a romantic relationship. He also loved Jesus. That was practically foreign to her, still.

He reached out his hand and laid it on the table, palm side up. His grin turned to a full-face smile. She reached out her hand and placed it in his. This was a new step in a relationship she vowed to take very slowly.

Having felt that her past romantic relationships had been a stumbling block for her faith, she was hesitant to act but also better studied on God's intention for marriage than she had ever been before.

> "Daughters of Jerusalem, I charge you: Do not arouse or awaken love until it so desires."
> Song of Solomon 8:4

Taking it slow seemed best but suddenly quite difficult. She was already in love with him, even though she did not want to admit it. She wanted to be like the apostle Paul and stay single forever so she could be devoted to Jesus only. It had become a point of pride in her.

"What are your biggest dreams for your life?" he asked thoughtfully.

"Oh, I don't know," she stated quietly. "Maybe you should go first. What are yours?"

With eyes bright and a suddenly serious posture, he shared what God had placed in His heart. She knew admiration must have been written on her face since it completely filled her.

Jesus, as I listen to him and find his dreams are the same as mine, what do I do? It is too soon to tell him I share the exact same dreams! It seems almost too good to be true. We just aren't that serious yet. What is this? That we have so much in common yet barely know each other?

"So, that's what is on my heart and mind to do. What about you?" he asked.

"Well… I would have to say that I have actually dreamed of doing the same since I was a little girl. I always read books or watched movies about this. It's my main goal in life."

His face showed his shock before he could correct it to a cooler, more comfortable affect. They were quiet and then awkwardly agreed to go ahead with ordering food, each desperate to change the subject.

As she walked in the door that evening, her mother asked how her day was. She hesitantly shared the common dreams she shared with this new friend. Her mother threw her hands in the air and said, "That's it! I knew you were going to marry him!"

There was no hiding the shocked expression she felt on her face as they both laughed and changed subjects. Every guy she had met the past year that had tried to pursue her had met her brick wall of self-protection. Now, she knew why.

> In their hearts humans plan their course, but the Lord establishes their steps.
> Proverbs 16:9

17

"I appreciate what you are trying to do, but you don't have the authority to do it."

She placed a reassuring hand on her child's shoulder. It was hard to rebuke a child with a helpful heart, but the stern spirit in the helpful nature needed softening. It was even harder as she recognized her own stern leanings in the demeanor of her child.

"I was just trying to help," the child quipped back with eyes searching her mother's face for approval.

"You were, but it is best to help in the ways help is needed. Sometimes, we can help without asking what kind of help is needed, but, most often, it is best to make sure the help you're offering is the help that is needed—the help that's helpful."

The child took in the lesson, gave a sincere "Yes ma'am" and grasped her mother's hand. Expressions of love were exchanged and playtime continued. The day went on.

Lord, You know I needed that lesson as much as she did. Help me to be helpful, to perceive the needs of the people in my life and meet them as You would have me to meet them.

How many times had she interjected herself into a situation, with the hope of helping, and found she was doing a job that wasn't hers to do? She had been learning to discern the needs of her community and to turn to prayer before action. Every person and place has needs, but knowing which needs were hers to meet had become her endeavor.

> "For we are God's handiwork, created in Christ Jesus to do good works, which God prepared in advance for us to do."
> Ephesians 2:10

Resting in her identity as a purposefully and masterfully created child of God, she was learning to look at each day with an expectation that God had work for her to do. He would help her to know her work in each moment.

"Mama, the timer is going off in the kitchen. Should I turn it off or hold the baby for you?" her daughter asked assertively.

She just smiled.

18

A soft hymn played in the background as the backdrop to this blessed scene. She reached for the hand that could no longer grip her own. The face of one she loved so dearly was once full and now sunken, hollow.

That really described her heart in this moment: sunken and hollow. She watched the person who had cared for her her whole life now needing care every moment. Nothing could ever fill the space in her life that would be left at the end of this day.

Oh Lord, am I selfish to ask for this to end? How can I want two things so much—more time but also less suffering?

Songs of blessed assurance and great faithfulness played on. Moment by moment new mercies she saw. That the Lord would show up at a time like this with His presence of peace seemed more than merciful. She truly could not find words for the comfort she felt.

> "Rejoice with those who rejoice; mourn with those who mourn."
> Romans 12:15

Father, thank You for leading by example. I know You are here with me and mourning. You are helping me know how to mourn with others like I never have before.

Her loved one seemed already gone but the jagged breath every few minutes reminded her that death was a process as much as a passing. The world might call this cruel—that life well lived would end in such an unlovely manner. Still, she felt comforted because she knew what lay ahead. She knew she was not alone. She knew this was not the end.

She leaned down and kissed the cool hand in her own. Whispered thanks escaped her lips for years of hugs and kisses, years of unconditional support and presence that seemed written in the wrinkles of that hand.

Unnoticed, the nurse had entered the room during this final exchange and now stood at her side. The silent presence at her side seemed to signal that this moment was coming to an end. A new song started softly behind them while the fullness of grief, mingled with the expectance of joy, washed over her.

> I stand amazed in the presence
> Of Jesus the Nazarene
> And wonder how He could love me
> A sinner, condemned, unclean
> O How Marvelous! O How Wonderful!
> And my song shall ever be
> O How Marvelous! O How Wonderful!
> Is my Savior's love for me![5]

---

5 Chris Tomlin. Lyrics to "I Stand Amazed (How Marvelous)." *Genius*, 2021, https://genius.com/Christomlin-i-stand-amazedhow-marvelous-lyrics.

19

Her colleague lifted her eyes just high enough to match her gaze and responded, "I just don't think God would do that."

She was never one to shy away from a spiritual discussion since becoming a follower of Jesus. This conversation started with discussions of home buying but led down a trail of trials littering the path of her colleague's life. They had progressed in recent weeks from "There is no real god" to "I just don't think God would do that".

She prayerfully considered what to say next, feeling compelled that wrong beliefs about God were as dangerous as no belief in God at all.

"God has done that and will do that again. In the Bible, we find that God is unchanging. He is still the God of the Old Testament as much as the New. His being is not dependent upon what we think about Him. He is. Period."

They pressed on to answer more questions: What does the Bible say about who God is? What has He done? Where did His wrath go after Jesus died and resurrected?

So many good questions would encourage a better understanding of this God she hoped her colleague would one day believe in.

As she navigated the discussion, she thought of her husband's admonishment to her. He repeated often that if one believes wrongly about God—thinking He is someone or something that He is not as opposed to who He says He is in His Word—then that belief is not actually believing in God. It may be believing in something but it is not belief in the One True God of the Bible.

"I'm not sure I can spend my whole life trying to know and understand everything about God. There is so much going on in my life and this job is a lot. I'll just have to think more about it later," her colleague said as she fastened the lids on her lunch containers.

She felt the Spirit of God open her heart with compassion and empathy. Reaching her hand across the table, she placed it on her colleague's hand and said, "Hey, this is a lot because God is a lot. He is more than I can understand or imagine. I don't believe in Him because of how vast He is or because of how much I know about Him. I believe in Him by faith. It is faith that saves us and brings us into a relationship with Him. Knowing Him can only come from knowing Him. It doesn't drain us or add to the already full bucket of life. It fills us and takes the weight from the bucket. Jesus made that possible. If you're going to think about this more, think about that instead of all you don't know or would need to learn."

Her colleague turned the palm of her hand up and held tightly.

"I believe what you're saying," she said. "I believe you believe it. Really, I haven't met many Christians like you. You've been so patient to talk with me when I have questions, and I appreciate that you have never made me feel like an enemy. I know you love me, friend. After each of these conversations, I leave knowing that I want Jesus. But, would He really want me?"

Tears brimmed in both of their eyes as she choked on her response to her colleague turned friend.

"Oh, He really would. He already does." she said. "It is true that no one can come to the Father except through Jesus. Right after Jesus said that, He also said that He did not come into the world to condemn the world but to save man through Himself! He did that because He knew you before you were formed in your mother's womb and wants His creation to be saved, to know Him! Our part in the equation is to believe that and be transformed, to ask forgiveness for all that has separated us from God—those things that have made you feel undesirable and unwanted—and then walk in His ways close to Him."

Her friend breathed a sigh that sounded like relief as she wiped her tears from her cheeks. Their beepers buzzed, a sign that their lunch was over and a patient needed them. They tidied the break room table quietly and quickly walked out to see what commotion was waiting for them at the desk.

There was more to be said but no time to say it. Her prayer flowed as her hands went to work.

Lord, You know her heart. Let her receive salvation with gladness. Thank you, Father, that the power for salvation is not in my eloquence but in the Gospel of Jesus Christ. You love her more than I do. Draw near to her and let her be saved.

For God so loved the world that he gave his one and only Son, that whoever believes in him shall not perish but have eternal life. For God did not send his Son into the world to condemn the world, but to save the world through him. Whoever believes in him is not condemned, but whoever does not believe stands condemned already because they have not believed in the name of God's one and only Son. This is the verdict: Light has come into the world, but people loved darkness instead of light because their deeds were evil. Everyone who does evil hates the light, and will not come into the light for fear that their deeds will be exposed. But whoever lives by the truth comes into the light, so that it may be seen plainly that what they have done has been done in the sight of God.
John 3:16-21

20

She hit her knees, again.

The feeling of her heart bowing to the ground as she felt her spirit lifted gave her a fresh breath for the next moment. It was another moment upon her face in prayer. She was desperate for the water of life to flow and sustain her. Christ's promise that those who drink of this water would never thirst again was still true, yet somehow she simultaneously felt parched.

The cash register rang as she took another step in the craft store check out line. Oh, how honestly on her face she could be in prayer in the spirit and yet be found amidst the aisles of home decor and fabric swatches.

It was the call of Christ in that moment that brought her to her face internally, *Abide in me. Remain in me. I am the vine.*

She was parched, not because the gardener had ceased to offer her living water, but because she had closed her mouth to the cup, shut off the valve to the spigot, and stuffed the well of life full of rocks.

Oh Father, how moment-by-moment is my need to care for my heart, my need to sit in Your sustaining presence. I rejoice in this work because I do not do it alone or by any of my own power! This is Your work in my heart. Forgive me for neglecting myself and Your commands – the very commands that Christ brought to life for life abundant in place of condemnation. Let Your living water flow through my heart to renew and refresh me.

> "Above all else, guard your heart, for everything you do flows from it."
> Proverbs 4:23

> "...Indeed, the water I give them will become in them a spring of water welling up to eternal life."
> John 4:14

She looked into the face of the cashier and made her usual comment about coming for one thing but leaving with more. How could she engage that conversation and feel as though she was truly on the ground in prayer, repentance, and returning to rest.

Indeed, she would be leaving the store with more than she expected. Returning. What a word. The call to returning—surrendered repentance—found her at the foot of Christ. Her chains were loosed, burdens lifted, and lungs filled with enough breath for the next moment. She would learn to abide there in Christ. She would learn to remain in Him. It would be her life's work and joy. It would be worth it.

> I am the true vine, and my Father is the gardener. He cuts off every branch in me that bears no fruit, while

every branch that does bear fruit he prunes so that it will be even more fruitful. You are already clean because of the word I have spoken to you. Remain in me, as I also remain in you. No branch can bear fruit by itself; it must remain in the vine. Neither can you bear fruit unless you remain in me.

I am the vine; you are the branches. If you remain in me and I in you, you will bear much fruit; apart from me you can do nothing. If you do not remain in me, you are like a branch that is thrown away and withers; such branches are picked up, thrown into the fire and burned. If you remain in me and my words remain in you, ask whatever you wish, and it will be done for you. This is to my Father's glory, that you bear much fruit, showing yourselves to be my disciples.

"As the Father has loved me, so have I loved you. Now remain in my love. If you keep my commands, you will remain in my love, just as I have kept my Father's commands and remain in his love. I have told you this so that my joy may be in you and that your joy may be complete.
     Johns 15:1-11

Afterward

Thank you for coming this far. It is my prayer that, as you have read this book, you have found a rhythm of praying and studying the Word of God that is infused into every moment of life. Writing these essays was a task I did not expect to need for myself, but, as I wrote them, the Lord showed me how He is present in each moment of my life and in constant communication with me. He has helped me return to Him in prayer better and better as my years of faith have progressed.

In the pages that follow, a question guide has been provided to study the Lord's lessons in these essays. These questions came from a dear friend who has led small groups and Bible studies over the years. I pray that, in reading these questions and thinking on your response, you would find a fresh breath of life in Christ. May the streams of living water be quickened to flow freely in you.

In the Love of Christ,
Hannah Burney Johnson

Discussion Guide

Questions posed by Esther Mollenhour for personal study or group discussion.

1

1. The news tried to steal her peace. What in your life steals your peace?

2. What do you do to guard your heart against those things?

3. She didn't just talk about watching less news or not letting it be the focus of her day. Her efforts sought solitude with the Lord. What concrete action step is the Lord prompting your heart to take right now?

4. Share that with your group/community and choose an accountability partner to walk with you in this.

2

1. What kind of witness are you?

2. Have you ever experienced unabashed faith? Is that how people would describe you?

3. What is your experience with moment-by-moment prompts from the Holy Spirit?

3

1. We often think that we must have it all together to be used by God, but 2 Cor. 12:9 tells us otherwise. Share about an experience when God used your weakness for His glory.

2. Take some time right now to ask the Lord what is grieving Him in your life. Partner up and confess your sin to the Lord and each other. Spend some time asking the Lord together what He's asking you to do next.

3. Use this week to encourage each other. Text or connect with one another each day what you're praying for each other.

4

1. Have you thought that becoming angry is a sin in and of itself? How does reframing that thought process through the Biblical truth – that anger itself isn't sin, but the way we act in anger may be sinful – help you move forward?

2. Share about a time like the one described when God used you to impact someone else in a way you didn't expect or realize.

3. Take time this week asking God to convict you of the ways you've sinned in your anger and ask Him how to redeem it.

5

1. How often does God prompt you to pray for a stranger? Have you been obedient in the past? Share about that.

2. Our prayers have eternal value. Who has prayed prayers that have impacted your life? Take time to thank them this week if you still have contact with them.

3. This story reminds us that sometimes we pray for people out loud and sometimes silently to ourselves. Be sensitive this week to the prompting of the Spirit to pray for people. Share your experience next time with the group.

6

1. Possessions can make us feel safe. This is often seen when something messes with our income or health and we're suddenly reminded that we're not in control. Ask yourself, would you feel the same about the Lord if you woke up tomorrow without your possessions? Without your health?

2. Share a time in your life when you were reminded that you aren't in control. Share how it impacted your relationship with the Lord.

3. This week ask the Father to remind you of the joy of your salvation, to renew your first love. Report back to the group the impact that these prayers have.

7

1. It is hard to think about in our humanity. But, we are human and our call to love each other doesn't have anything to do with how well others love us. This calling has to do with how obedient we are to the Father's call to love others.

2. Think about the hardest person in your life to love, what changes when you shift your thoughts to obedience to the Father? What if the reward is not how the other person treats us in response, but if it is "well done, good and faithful servant?"

3. Ask God what He loves about the other person and ask Him to let you see them through His eyes.

4. Talk about how it would impact your relationships for the basis of each relationship to be what the Father is calling you to do instead of how the other person treats you.

(Reminder: Boundaries and Safety within relationships are essential. Practicing godly relationships should not dismiss or allow abuse. If you feel unsafe in a relationship or are a victim of abuse in any form, reach out to the National Domestic Abuse Hotline at 800.799.SAFE (7233). We are praying for you, specifically, as we write this.)

8

1. It can seem more daring, obedient, and sacrificial to travel and serve (and it has very unique sacrifices) but the most sacrificial serving can happen anywhere. What is the most sacrificial serving God is calling to you right now?

2. Do you spend much time thinking about how this world is not our home? How does that impact you?

9

1. When was the last time you felt like you were not enough?

2. God never asked us to be enough, He just asked for willingness and surrender. What thing is stressing you out the most right now? How would surrendering it to the Lord impact you?

3. This week, practice taking stressful thoughts captive to the Lord. Picture yourself, open handed, giving them to the Lord like a little child. Report back next week how that affected your mental health and outlook.

10

1. Next things are hard. What "next thing" are you navigating right now?

2. How does it affect the way you're tackling the "next thing" to know that you're not alone?

3. We saw that Moses' inability to speak didn't matter; what mattered was what God was calling him to do. Partner up and share what you believe God is calling you to do. Share what "speaking" is for you. Remember, these things don't have to seem possible by human standards, in fact they probably won't. Text the prayers you're praying for each other each day as you take your next step.

11

1. Share about one of the most impactful friendships of your life.

2. What makes a good friend?

3. How are you loving your friends well?

4. Take a few minutes to pray and ask the Father what friend needs your extra attention this week. Pray for them each morning and follow the Holy Spirit on any prompts He stirs.

5. Think through how God wants to use you in friendships. What steps do you need to take to get there?

12

Scripture tells us to "be holy as I am holy" – does that even sound possible? **The truth is that, without Jesus, it isn't possible.** When we confess that we are sinners in need of a Savior, we have been saved. We're covered, the work is done for our salvation, but His refinement of our character carries on.

Sinful actions and behaviors are still harmful to us. In fact, since we have become new creations in Christ, the Holy Spirit is actively, kindly, calling us to repentance.

1. Partner up and share the thing in your life that is bringing the most conviction. You'll know what it is because it makes you the most uncomfortable when you ask the Holy Spirit to reveal it.

   As you receive confessions from each other, know that you are in a sacred space. Your job is not to rescue each other out of the place of conviction. It might seem nice to say things like, "me too," or "that's understandable," but when the Holy Spirit is doing a work it is not our job to undo it. It is our job to join them in prayer. By responding with prayer and the redemptive truth of Scripture we are partnering with the Father in the heart work that He is doing.

2. Repentance is a beautiful gift of our Christian journey— it frees you from underlying tension and heartache. Pray for each other this week that when conviction comes, we wouldn't be defensive, but that it would bring us to our knees. What do you need to take it to the Great Physician just like you would take an illness to our primary care doctors? Text or call each other with encouragement this week.

13

1. Think back to a time when someone misused the Bible against you. Close your eyes for a second. Be brave to go back. There is redemption ahead. Sit in the tenderness of those feelings without sharing them, for a bit. Now, go around the room and take turns speaking truth from God's Word about the person to your left.

2. Your "Christian Counsel" is brave enough not to rescue you from conviction and wise enough to speak truth when you're walking in shame. Who is this in your life?

3. Spend time each morning this week asking the Lord to reveal untruths that have been spoken over you that you've believed. Then spend some time in His word soaking up the truth.

14

1. Community in the Spirit happens when we take the focus off of ourselves and put it on the Father. How often have you avoided a situation because you were expecting awkwardness and a lack of connection?

2. What is your least favorite social situation or setting?

3. What if, instead of focusing on how we feel, we started considering that the situation might be a divine opportunity? Think back to when you met one of your closest friends, did you go into that time expecting a life changing interaction?

4. Do you have an experience to share like the one described in this piece?

5. Can you share an example of when you've been "at the right place at the right time" or has someone been there for you right when you needed him or her? Share those experiences and thank God for His divine appointments.

15

1. It feels counter intuitive, but stopping to rest and refocus on God can be the most productive thing we do in a day. Have you found that to be true?

2. What is your best practice for resting and abiding? How are you feeling convicted to take that a step further? Or possibly refashion your time?

16

1. Tell the story of a time when God clearly had you moving forward through a door you thought you'd closed or maybe one you never thought you'd go through.

2. How do you process such decisions?

3. How can you tell when God is giving you direction?

4. When this story starts, she has released something to the Lord (something that she had not handled well in the past). Is there something in your life that needs to be released so God can do His redemptive work?

17

Healthy serving/helping comes solely from a motivation to be obedient and follow a prompt from the Holy Spirit. **We are not responsible for the outcome of the situation — our only responsibility is obedience.**

1. Have you ever helped someone, making various sacrifices, only to have them be ungrateful?

2. Now reframe that situation. Ask the Father, *Was I obedient in the time and/or resources that I gave?* If the answer is yes, then their response does not matter. Only the response of the Father to you matters.

3. Break into groups of 2-3 people and share with each other the thing (i.e. person, situation, etc) in your life that seems to be demanding the most help from you.

4. Set aside the most obvious "help" that comes to mind and spend time praying for each other asking God what obedience looks like. Once you've done that, release the outcome to Him.

18

1. The deepest grief in our lives is both the hardest road we've ever walked and, miraculously, the hardest evidence that God is real. Share about one of the greatest losses of your life.

2. How has God shown Himself faithful even if you couldn't see it at the time?

3. What did the situation teach you about mourning with others?

4. What change did it bring about in you?

19

1. For you, what is the most intimidating part about sharing the Gospel?

2. What misconceptions of God have you encountered from other people?

3. What is the hardest thing about God to explain? What makes you choose Him anyway?

4. **The truth is that the power for salvation is not in our eloquence, but in the Gospel of Jesus Christ.** How does this impact you?

<u>20</u>

1. Break up into groups of 2-3 people and spend a few minutes asking the Father in prayer what He wants to "cut off" from your life because it's not bearing fruit. Share what He showed you.

2. Describe what abiding in Christ looks like. What is your experience with having living water flow through you? Write down your thoughts and share, as you feel led.

3. Are you feeling convicted about shifting something in your daily routine and thought processes so that you can abide daily?

For your final discussion time or prayerful reflection on these chapters, revisit the Preface. May these final questions help give form and application to all God has shown you in this book.

Preface

1. Break into groups of 2-3 people. Spend some time thanking God for the work He has done in this study.

2. Share with each other the growth that you've seen in them. Be bold to share the things the Spirit is asking of you, not just what your flesh is comfortable with. You never know how powerfully God can use the words of life we speak over each other.

3. Take some time in prayer asking God to make evident the next act of obedience that He's stirring in your heart. It may be confirmation of something you've felt for awhile, or it could be something new. **You'll know what it is because, most likely, it will make your heart race because it is miles outside of your comfort zone.** You may feel ill equipped because, just like the author, He will bring it out of your weakness. That way, *you will never forget that it was through His strength and not your own that it happened.* In faith, speak it out loud.

4. Pray for each other and journal what takes place so that you can look back at His faithfulness. The prayers and practical steps of walking these things out together will carry far beyond today.

Acknowledgments

This book is an overflow of what God has been placing in my heart to write over the past few years. In 2019, I knew that I needed consecration in prayer and fasting for something I would write in the days ahead. Without knowing what that writing would be, I focused on nearness to God and doing His work each day. He was and is near. With that in mind, it is Him I thank first.

Thank You, Father in heaven, for the Word of God that lives in me. Thank you for my salvation – this beautiful act of Christ knowing and pursing me that gives belief and relationship with You. Thank You that salvation is open to all who would believe. Thank You for walking with me, step by step, in the life of belief. Thank you for giving me the words to say and write here. May they achieve Your purposes.

Thank you to my husband. Billy, you pastor and lead me. Thank you for always being my listening ear, my confidant, my personal comedian, and my best friend. Thank you for telling me to sit down and write at just the right moment. You are the love of my life and I will follow you wherever the Lord calls us.

Thank you to my daughters. Each of you have taught me more about the Father's love than any Bible study ever could. You are each unique and beautiful, strong and gentle. May I help you grow in Christ for all the days ahead.

Thank you to my mother. Your life is a testimony of relying on God in prayer. Thank you for showing me what it looks like to see every purpose through to the end, in as much as you have the ability to do so. You inspire me.

Thank you to my father. You wrote from Proverbs 9:10 in the front of my first real Bible, "The fear of the Lord is the beginning of wisdom…" It has been my true joy to understand this better each day. Thank you for instilling in me reverence and dedication to the Word of God.

Thank you to my Aunt Amy. You often inspire next steps in my life. Whether it is a word of encouragement in my steps in motherhood or proofreading an entire book on my behalf, God blesses me through your faithfulness. I thank the Lord for you.

Thank you to my family. I have an army of loving people that I am honored to call family by birth and by marriage. To my step-parents, my siblings, my grandparents, my family-in-love, and beyond, each of you add to the fullness of my life in every way.

Thank you to my first readers. This mighty group of prayerful women tested and discerned my words in such beautiful, edifying ways. Thank you for your time, prayer, and response.

Thank you to Esther Mollenhour. You prayerfully wrote the questions included here as a response to reading these words. May God continue the powerful work He is always doing in your devoted heart. It's my privilege to walk alongside you, even from afar.

Thank you to Terrie Starkey. Your painting of stacked tomatoes on a warm summer day has traveled the world with our family as a treasure. I know just why the Lord led me to you for the beautiful cover art on this book.

Thank you to Mr. McKay. You read the first story that I wrote about my faith during my senior year of high school. It was an assignment to write a love story. You said, "This is good." I balked because it was a storied moment of really knowing God. Now, here are many stories to share for the same reason. Really knowing God is good.

My final thanks are for One Church. God showed me on my first Sunday serving there that this book was meant for this time because I would share it with you. Thank you Pastors Blake and Mike for helping me achieve this by your encouragement and prayerful belief in what God has given me to say. Thank you to Ally for loving me and leading me from the early days of my marriage. Thank you to the people of One Church who have welcomed us in with open arms and hearts to such beautiful, real fellowship. God bless you, all.

> In the Love of Christ,
> Hannah Burney Johnson